STORY OF
BASEBALL
COLORING BOOK

E. Lisle Reedstrom

Dover Publications, Inc.
Mineola, New York

At Dover Publications we're committed to producing books in an earth-friendly manner and to helping our customers make greener choices.

Manufacturing books in the United States ensures compliance with strict environmental laws and eliminates the need for international freight shipping, a major contributor to global air pollution. And printing on recycled paper helps minimize our consumption of trees, water and fossil fuels.

The text of this book was printed on paper made with 50% post-consumer waste and the cover was printed on paper made with 10% post-consumer waste. At Dover, we use Environmental Paper Network's Paper Calculator to measure the benefits of these choices, including: the number of trees saved, gallons of water conserved, as well as air emissions and solid waste eliminated.

Courier Corporation, the manufacturer of this book, owns the Green Edition Trademark.

Please visit the product page for *Story of Baseball Coloring Book* at www.doverpublications.com to see a detailed account of the environmental savings we've achieved over the life of this book.

A Note on Coloring

The colors used on the covers of this book are "freestyle" examples. For greater historical accuracy in coloring please read the following information and the instructions at the end of each caption.

Except where specifically stated otherwise, all shoes and belts are black; and all caps, pants, cap lettering, cap insignias, shirts, socks and (under)sweaters (usually seen covering the forearms) are white. Gloves can be any shade of brown. Bats are yellow to tan in color.

In the case of socks, a crescent-shaped area is often found above the tongue of the shoe and above the heel. These areas are to be left white—they are the understocking beneath the sock. These white patches tend to increase in size as the book goes on, especially after page 37. Where used, the number of a sock stripe is counted from the top of the sock.

Bibliographical Note

Story of Baseball Coloring Book is a new work, first published by Dover Publications, Inc., in 1991, and revised and updated in 2012.

International Standard Book Number

ISBN-13: 978-0-486-26748-7
ISBN-10: 0-486-26748-2

Manufactured in the United States by RR Donnelley
26748216   2016
www.doverpublications.com

INTRODUCTION

Baseball, as most of those reading this page must realize, is America's national game. That is not an official designation; rather, it reflects the fact that baseball has grown up along with the growing United States. It has contributed an irreplaceable tradition of excellence and heroism in sport, with many colorful figures and memorable events that have become undeniable elements of American history and identity, to a degree far exceeding that of any other sport. Even today, names from the past like Ty Cobb, Babe Ruth, Roberto Clemente and the Brooklyn Dodgers evoke a resonant complex of emotions that practically borders on the mystical. And, in spite of all the changes that have occurred in the game within the past 200 years, it is still pretty much the same "playing at base" enjoyed by American soldiers at Valley Forge. It is a living, essentially unbroken, tradition, extending through the development of intercity competition in the mid-nineteenth century up to the present.

One of the most visible aspects of baseball as a continuing tradition is an array of statistics and records, all those numbers that are at the heart of the game. When a major league player takes up a bat, a glove or a ball, he is, in a sense, not only competing against an opposing team, but also against over 100 years of baseball achievements *and* against the performance of contemporaries on his own and other teams. Who can say what is a greater thrill for a player—to boost one's team to the World Series or to, say, win the season's title for most home runs? It is an impossible choice, one that is best resolved when both the group and the individual are rewarded for their efforts. All of this is why the reader will find so many numbers in this book. They are the very essence of baseball—an objective basis of comparison in the face of partisan fervor and fierce loyalties.

The players in this book have been chosen to represent the ongoing story of baseball; they are not intended to set forth "the greatest ballplayers of all time." They were players who made a distinctive and individual contribution to the game, and they all happened to be great baseball players. All but two of this group of forty-five are officially enshrined in the National Baseball Hall of Fame. Smoky Joe Wood has an unusual set of records that is worth noting as indicative of a great talent, even if he lacked the staying power that warrants inclusion in the Hall. Pete Rose, without a doubt one of baseball's greats, will only be eligible for the Hall when his banishment from the game (incurred through tax and gambling violations) is lifted.

Baseball may have lost some of its bigger-than-life mythic quality since the days when Ruth and Gehrig graced the diamond, but it still preserves the best blend of team and individual aspirations in sports. For this reason, we can expect baseball to have a bright future, with room to spare for the mythic as well.

BRIAN DOHERTY

Denton T. (Cy) Young (1867–1955), named "O'Cyclone" for his fastball, pitched for Cleveland and St. Louis in the National League (NL) and then the Red Sox and the Indians in the American League (AL). Cy's productivity was astonishing during his twenty-two-year career. He won more than 20 games each year from 1891 to 1904 (with a slump of 19 in 1900), with a 35-10 won-lost record in 1895. Overall, Cy won 511 games (the all-time record) and pitched three no-hitters. Cy Young is often considered the greatest pitcher in the history of baseball. The highest award in pitching is named for him. *Cap, shirt, pants: gray. Socks, sweater: navy blue.*

John J. (Little Napoleon) McGraw (1873–1934) began his major league career as a star third baseman for the Baltimore Orioles. With his help, the Orioles became the NL champions three times
in the 1890s. In 1902, he accepted the position of manager for the New York Giants, a spot he held
for thirty years. Because of his remarkable leadership abilities, the Giants won ten pennants and
three World Championships. McGraw was virtually unmatched for arrogance and feistiness—and for
managerial excellence. He was the model for all the temperamental and pugnacious managers that
would follow. *Cap and shirt insignias: blue. Visor, socks (top and bottom): violet.*

George E. (Rube) Waddell (1876–1914) was a strong left-handed pitcher for Philadelphia's Athletics and other teams. He had one of the best curveballs of his day as well as a blazing fastball. He established many different records in his time. Rube held the record for strikeouts in a single game and his season record of 349 stood untouched until 1965. In a 1908 game, he turned back the White Sox with a single hit. Rube is one of only ten AL pitchers to have won the Triple Crown for pitching: leading the league in wins, ERA and strikeouts in a given year. A true eccentric, Waddell would often be found to have gone fishing when he was supposed to be pitching a game. *Cap, socks: black.*

Sam (Wahoo Sam) Crawford (1880–1968) was placed with the Detroit Tigers in an outfield position in 1899. He was one of the hardest hitters of his time. Not only did he hit home runs, but he hit triples with greater regularity than any other player in the annals of baseball. He holds the all-time career record with 309 three-baggers. He was the first player to lead both leagues in homers (1901, Cincinnati: 16; 1908, Detroit: 7). Wahoo Sam finished his ball-playing days with a .309 lifetime batting average, 2,964 hits and three RBI (runs batted in) titles. *Socks, visor: dark blue.*

Christy (Matty) Mathewson (1880–1925) had his first full season in the majors in 1901, pitching for the Giants. That year the right-hander won 20 and lost 17. After a slump in 1902, he came back and over the next twelve years consistently won 22 or more per season, reaching a peak in 1908 with 37 wins against ll losses, setting an NL record for season wins. In 1909, his earned run average (ERA) was an amazing 1.14. He led the NL five times in ERA and five times in strikeouts. Matty had at his disposal a great arsenal of pitches, including a notorious fadeaway (a.k.a. screwball). *Cap, socks: navy blue. Sweater: light tan. Lettering on shirt: black.*

Ty Cobb (1886–1961) began his career in center field for Detroit, later joining the Athletics. Following his first year, the aggressive Cobb never batted below .320. His twenty-four years in the majors (1905-1928) produced the following figures: 3,034 games, 4,191 hits (#2 all-time), 297 triples (#2 all-time), 2,244 runs scored (#2 all-time), 892 stolen bases (#4 all-time), 1,937 RBI (#6 all-time) and a .367 batting average (#1 all-time). The statistics are clear, Cobb was one of the game's immortals and probably the most purely competitive ballplayer ever. For many, it is a toss-up whether Ty Cobb or Babe Ruth was the greatest offensive performer in baseball history. *Socks, collar: black. Sweater: light tan.*

Grover Alexander (1887–1950) began pitching for the Phillies in 1911. His 373 career victories tie him with Christy Mathewson for all-time lead among NL pitchers. For six seasons straight, his ERA never topped 1.91. He pitched a record 16 shutouts in 1916. Alexander led the NL in wins six times, strikeouts six times and ERA five times (winning a record-tying 3 Triple Crowns). He averaged better than 27 wins a year his first seven years in the majors. In 1917 he was signed to the Cubs and in 1918 served abroad in World War I. Upon his return, he started drinking heavily, ruining his career by 1930, but not before additional brilliant seasons, e.g., 1926 with the World Champion Cardinals. *Stripes on cap: white. Cap, socks, letter on shirt: red. Shirt, pants: gray.*

Eddie Collins (1887–1951) was second baseman for the Chicago White Sox from 1915 to 1926. Collins came to the majors as a nineteen-year-old shortstop with Connie Mack's Athletics in 1906. Two years later, he took over second base. Collins ranks seventh in all-time stolen bases (743). His lifetime batting average was .333 with a high of .369 in 1920. He is a member of the select 28-member 3,000-hit club. He played in six World Series with a Series average of .328 in 34 games. Collins retired in 1930. *Elephant: white. Sweater: gray. Socks (middle stripe): black.*

Walter Johnson (1887–1946) was one of the most beloved of all ballplayers. Johnson was the fastest pitcher that ever lived—on the mound he was regarded something the way Babe Ruth was at the bat. Almost all who faced him considered him the best pitcher in history. His lifetime strikeouts totalled 3,508. His 113 shutouts remain the highest total in major league annals. He pitched for twenty-one years (1907-1927) with the Washington Nationals, winning 416 games, more than any other pitcher in this century (quite impressive when one considers Washington's frequent residence in the AL basement). His career ERA in nearly 6,000 innings was 2.17. He won 20 or better twelve times and nabbed the hurling Triple Crown three times. *Socks (top stripe), cap, "W" on arms: navy blue. Shirt, pants: gray.*

Joe (Smoky Joe) Wood (1889–1985) was a pitcher for the Red Sox (1908-1915) and outfielder for the Indians (1917-1922). In 1912 he won 34 games (including 16 straight), lost only 5, struck out 258, pitched a league-leading 10 shutouts and had an ERA of 1.91, perhaps the most remarkable season for any pitcher ever. During the World Series against the Giants, he won 3 more, including the final game against Mathewson. In 1915, Wood went 15-5 with a league-leading 1.49 ERA. Giving up the mound, Wood played outfield for Cleveland for several years, batting .366 (in 66 games) in 1921. *Socks (middle stripe), shirt letters: red.*

George Sisler (1893-1973) played ball with the St. Louis Browns between 1915 and 1927 as a pitcher and first baseman. He was quickly recognized as one of the finest first basemen in the league, although he is best remembered as a hitter. The peak of his career was 1920-1922, when he batted .407, .371 and .420, leading the AL in 1920 and 1922. In 1920 he racked up 257 hits, a single-season record until 2004. In each of these peak years, he drove in more than 100 runs and hit 18 triples. In four years he led the AL in stolen bases. In 1922 he hit in 41 straight games. Sisler retired in 1930. *Socks (top stripe), shirt letters, visor, belt: brown. Shirt, pants: tan.*

George Herman (Babe) Ruth (1895–1948) was, by popular acclaim, the greatest baseball player of all time. He is most remembered for his many home runs (714), but he actually came to the majors in 1914 as a great pitcher for the Red Sox. He led the AL in pitching in 1916 with an ERA of 1.75! He began hitting homers in 1918 with 11—the next year he hit 29. Needing money, Boston sold Babe to the Yankees for $125,000 (*and* a loan) in 1920. That year he knocked 54 out of the park and the "King of Homers" was born, blasting away the "deadball era" of dominant pitching. He hit 59 home runs in 1921 and in 1927 became the first to hit 60. Ruth led the AL in hitting with .378 in 1924. Babe retired after 28 games with the Boston Braves in 1935. *Socks (middle stripe), shirt letters: red. Shirt, pants: light gray.*

Bill Terry (1898–1989) entered major league baseball in 1923 with the New York Giants after playing for Southern teams for nine years. He was a great first baseman and held the title for best hitting in 1930 with an average of .401, the last National Leaguer to hit the .400 mark. That year, Terry also had 254 hits (still the NL record), 23 homers and 129 RBI. Terry continued playing first base for the Giants with much success. In 1932 he succeeded John McGraw as manager. He piloted his team to the National League pennant three times and the World Championship in 1933. *Insignias, visor, first and third thin sock stripes: red. Other thin sock stripes: blue.*

Harold (Pie) Traynor (1899–1972) was a shortstop and third baseman for Pittsburgh from 1920 through 1937. Although Pie was a lifetime .320 hitter, it was his fielding that fans preferred to talk about. He led National League third basemen in putouts seven times, a record, as is his lifetime total of 2,291. Pie batted over .300 from 1925 to 1930, cresting with the latter year's .366. Not a home-run hitter, he did knock in more than 100 runs seven times. In 1923 he led the NL in triples with 19. He struck out only 278 times from 1920 to 1937, fanning an incredibly low seven times in 540 at bat in 1929. *Shirt letters, cap, socks (top stripe), piping: navy blue. Cap letter: red.*

Robert (Lefty) Grove (1900–1975) was a fastball pitcher for the Athletics and Red Sox from 1925 through 1941. Lefty ranked as the leading pitcher of the American League in 1928 (24-8), 1930 (28-5),1931 (31-4) and 1933 (24-8) in wins. He led in strikeouts his first seven years. He led the AL in ERA nine times and his four straight ERA titles are still an American League record. Lefty joined the Red Sox in 1934, where he earned four more ERA titles after turning thirty-five. In 1941 Lefty gained his 300th and final big league victory. *Cap, socks (first and third stripes): dark blue. Socks (bottom half), shirt letters, cap letter: red.*

Leon Allen (Goose) Goslin (1900–1971) came to the Washington club in 1921 as an outfielder and rapidly established himself as the game's premier RBI man. During his first full season, he drove in 99 runs and in eleven of the next thirteen seasons had 100 or more runs batted in. He beat Babe Ruth's RBI total in 1924 with 129. From 1924 to 1927 Goose hit .344, .334, .354 and .334. In 1928 he led the league with .379. His personal high came in 1930 with 37 home runs and 138 RBI. He was instrumental in winning the 1934 and 1935 pennants as well as the 1935 World Series for Detroit. *Socks (top portion), belt: brown. Cap, shirt, pants: light brown.*

Al (Bucketfoot) Simmons (1902–1956) was a right-handed hitter for the Philadelphia Athletics from 1924 through 1932 and played outfield. Seven other teams were his home from 1933 through 1944. Bucketfoot was one of the most lethal right-handed hitters of all time, with a lifetime batting average of .334 and a total of 2,927 hits, including 307 home runs. In 1930 and 1931 he won back-to-back batting titles with .381 and .390. In four World Series, he batted .329 and pulled 6 home runs. Al concluded his big league career in 1944. *Cap, piping: dark blue. Shirt, pants: gray. Insignias: red.*

Lou Gehrig (1903–1941) was a power-hitting left-handed first baseman for the Yankees from 1923 through 1939. He played 2,130 consecutive games (a record broken by Cal Ripkin, Jr. in 1995) from 1935 to 1939, earning him the nickname "Iron Horse." For thirteen straight seasons, Lou drove in more than 100 runs and in seven of these drove in over 150. His 184 RBI in 1931 is a league record. In his seven World Series, he had a batting average of .361, with 10 home runs and 35 RBI. Lou suffered from a sclerosis (known to this day as "Lou Gehrig's Disease") that finally took his life. One of the best baseball movies, The *Pride of the Yankees,* was about him. In his life, Gehrig lived up to the title. *Socks, cap: navy blue.*

Carl Hubbell (1903–1988), a great left-handed screwball pitcher for the New York Giants, had a brilliant sixteen-year pitching career (1928-1943). The soft-spoken Hubbell won 253 games in his lifetime. He led the National League in wins and in ERA three times. He led the league in strikeouts in 1937 with 159. In 1933 he successfully pitched 10 shutouts. In the 1934 All-Star game, Hubbell struck out Babe Ruth, Lou Gehrig, Jimmie Foxx, Al Simmons and Joe Cronin in a row. *Cap lettering, socks (thin stripes): orange. Shirt, pants: light gray. Rest of socks, shirt letters, cap: black.*

Bill Dickey (1907–1993) was a catcher for the Yankees from 1928 through 1943. In 1936 Bill's batting average was .362, which remained the highest ever for a catcher until 2009. During his career, he batted .300 or higher eleven times, with a lifetime mark of .313. He also holds the AL record for going through a full season (1931, 125 games) without a passed ball. For four consecutive seasons (1936-1939) he had more than 100 runs per season. He was behind the plate with eight Yankee pennant winners. After serving in the Navy in World War II, Bill took over as Yankee manager for most of the 1946 season. *Cap, socks: navy blue. Shirt, pants: light gray. Padding: brown.*

Jimmie Foxx (1907—1967) was a right-handed first baseman for the Philadelphia Athletics and Boston Red Sox from 1925 to 1942. He was only eighteen when he was purchased by the Athletics in 1925. He led the AL in runs scored in 1932 and batting in 1933, with an average of .356 in 149 games. Foxx led the league in homers four times and is seventeenth on the all-time list. He began as a catcher but ended up at first. In 1935 Connie Mack sold him to the Red Sox. Foxx's best year was 1932, in which he hit 58 homers. *Shirt, pants: gray. Cap, piping, socks (top portion): dark blue.*

Ernie Lombardi (1908–1977) held the position of catcher for the Cincinnati Reds, the New York Giants and other teams from 1931 through 1947. When he came to bat, he sent the shortstops and the third basemen back to the outfield grass. Thanks to his bulletlike line drives, he won two batting titles with a .342 average in 1938 and .330 in 1942. His lifetime average was .306, Lombardi having hit over .300 in ten seasons. *Padding: brown. Visor, sweater: red. Cap: dark blue.*

Luke Appling (1909–1991) was a shortstop for the Chicago White Sox from 1930 to 1950. In seventeen seasons he batted over .300. In 1936 he reached the heights of his career with a league-leading .388 average, the highest ever for a shortstop. In that year, he also had 204 hits and drove in 128 runs. He hit .328 in 1943 for another AL title. In 1949 the forty-year-old Appling hit .301; his lifetime figure was .310. He led shortstops in assists seven times, an American League record. Appling was voted greatest White Sox player ever in the 1970s. *Sweater, shirt letters, cap: black. Piping, sleeve stripes: red. Shirt, pants: very light tan.*

Hank Greenberg (1911–1986) was an outfielder and first baseman for the Detroit Tigers and Pittsburgh Pirates from 1939 to 1947. In both positions, Hank was brilliant as a performer for the Tiger's pennant drives. He hit .357 in the 1940 World Series against the Reds, driving in 6 runs. His 1940 average was .340, with 150 runs batted in, 41 home runs and 50 two-baggers, giving him the crown for the latter three categories. He hit 331 home runs in twelve seasons. Hank finished his career with the Pirates in 1947. *Socks, sweater, cap, shirt letters: navy blue. Shirt, pants: gray.*

Dizzy Dean (1911–1974) was employed by the St. Louis Cardinals as a right-handed pitcher. From 1932 to 1935 he led the NL in strikeouts. In 1934 he broke through with a 30-7 record, the NL's last 30-game winner. That year, Dizzy led in wins, winning percentage, complete games, strikeouts and shutouts. At twenty-five years of age, he was the greatest drawing card in baseball. In 1937 he was selected to start the All-Star game for the NL. Dean's toe was broken by a fierce line drive. Instead of heading for the bench, he continued playing. In pain, he used an unusual motion as he pitched, causing a permanent arm injury that effectively ended his career. *Shirt, pants: tan. Cap line; first, third, seventh and ninth sock stripes: red. Socks (middle stripe): blue.*

Joe (The Yankee Clipper) DiMaggio (1914–1999) was a right-handed outfielder with the New York Yankees from 1936 to 1951. He won the AL batting title in 1939 and 1940, with averages of .381 and .352 respectively. His outstanding fielding abilities matched his batting prowess. Within a five-year period (1937-1941) he displayed a cumulative batting average of .352 with 691 runs batted in. "Joltin' Joe" led the league in home runs in 1937 (46) and 1948 (39), homering 30 or more times in seven seasons. Joe was not only a player who set records, he was highly respected and set standards for the game. *Sweater, socks, cap, insignia: navy blue. Shoulder patch: red.*

Ted Williams (1918–2002) was one of the most outstanding rookies with the 1939 Boston Red Sox. He stayed with the Red Sox until 1960. Ted developed a studious approach to the art and science of hitting and became one of the greatest hitters of all time. He was the last player to hit .400 or above and remains high on the all-time lists for career home runs, batting average and RBI. He was a Triple Crown winner in 1942 (.356, 36 homers, 137 RBI) and 1947 (.343, 32, 114). *First and third sock stripes, cap, sweater, shirt letters: navy blue. Socks (bottom portion): red.*

Bob Feller (1918–2010) was employed as a pitcher by the Cleveland Indians from 1936 to 1956. At seventeen years of age, he made newspaper headlines and at eighteen, he was a regular big league starter. At nineteen, he was breaking records. At twenty-three, Bob had already recorded seasons of 24-9, 27-11 and 25-13. He led the American League three consecutive years in wins and strikeouts. Military service interrupted his record breaking for four years. Afterwards, Feller had his greatest season (1946), setting a new major league strikeout record with 348, winning 26 games, 10 of them shutouts. *Sweater: gray. Socks, cap: navy blue. Cap letter: red.*

Jackie Robinson (1919–1972) was a fine fielder and a deadly clutch hitter. He played for the Brooklyn Dodgers and was the first black man in the majors in modern times. Defiant, but never reckless,
he stole home nineteen times in his career. As a twenty-eight-year-old rookie, in 1947, he hit .297
and led the league in stolen bases. In 1949 he had his greatest year, batting a league-leading .342,
driving in 124 runs, getting 203 hits and again leading in stolen bases. That year, Jackie was voted the
National League's Most Valuable Player (MVP). During his ten years with the Dodgers, he hit over
.300 six times. *Socks, sweater, shirt letters, cap: navy blue.*

Roy Campanella (1921–1993) came to the spring training camp of the Dodgers in 1948 and remained for ten years. He was a powerful hitter and a flawless defensive catcher. Roy was voted the National League's Most Valuable Player in 1951, 1953 and 1955. Playing 144 games in 1953, he batted .312, hit 41 home runs and drove in a league-leading 142 runs. In 1958 Roy was involved in a car accident that ended his baseball career. Paralyzed from the neck down, he spent the rest of his life in a wheelchair. *Socks, sweater, shirt letters, cap: navy blue. Shirt, pants: light gray.*

Lawrence Peter (Yogi) Berra (born 1925) was a catcher for the Yankees from 1949 to 1963. In the seventeen full seasons that Yogi was with the Yankees, they won fourteen pennants and ten World Championships. He had ten straight years with 20 or more home runs. A power hitter, he struck out just 12 times in 597 at bat in 1950. Yogi became one of the shrewdest handlers of pitchers and most adept of defensive catchers, once handling 950 consecutive chances in 148 games without an error—setting two major league records. He was voted AL MVP in 1951, 1954 and 1955. As a manager, Yogi won one pennant each for the Mets and the Yankees. *Socks, cap, sweater: navy blue.*

Duke Snider (1926–2011) was a great defensive center fielder for the Dodgers from 1947 through 1962. From 1953 through 1957, he connected for 40 or more home runs, a National League record. In 1953 he batted .336, in 1954 .341. In 1955 he led the league with 136 RBI and in 1956 with 43 homers. He was one of the most powerful hitters in World Series history. In six Series with the Dodgers, he hit 11 home runs, fourth in all-time Series homers. Twice, in 1952 and 1955, he hit 4 round-trippers in a Series. Snider finished up his career with 407 home runs. *Sweater, socks, piping, cap: navy blue.*

Ernie Banks (born 1931) was a shortstop and first baseman for the Chicago Cubs from 1953 to 1971. He was known as "Mr. Sunshine" during his nineteen-year career with the Cubs. His only disappointment was never playing in a World Series: he holds the modern records for most games (2,528) and most homers (512) by a player never to see Series action. Ernie hit 512 home runs for the Cubs and in 1958 and 1959 he led the National League in RBI, and was named NL MVP both years. The 47 home runs he knocked out in 1958 established a new record for most home runs by a shortstop. Ernie will always be remembered for his enthusiastic "Let's play two today!" Voted greatest Cub player of all time. *Cap letter: red. Socks, sweater, cap: navy blue.*

Willie Mays (born 1931) was a center fielder for San Francisco from 1951 to 1972. During Willie's first few games, he went hitless ... then came his first hit in the majors—a long homer off Warren Spahn. After that, his career took off, making and breaking records all the way. In 1954, after returning from military service, he was the NL's MVP: he hit 41 homers, drove in 110 runs and compiled a .345 batting average. In 1965 he won MVP a second time. By the time Willie had finished playing, he had hit 660 home runs. Willie was one of the greatest players ever to play the game and will always be recalled for his running over-the-shoulder catch in the 1954 World Series. *Shirt, pants: light gray. Cap insignia, piping: orange. Sweater, cap, sock: black.*

Mickey Mantle (1931–1995) was an outfielder for the Yankees. Mickey was one of the toughest and most dynamic players in baseball history in spite of injuries and pain that plagued him throughout his career. His greatest season was 1956, when he became the sixth Triple Crown winner in AL history with a .353 batting average, 52 home runs and 130 RBI. In 1961 he hit 54 homers, runner-up to teammate Roger Maris' then-record 61. He was AL MVP in 1956, 1957 and 1962. He led four times in home runs, once in triples, six times in runs scored and three times in slugging average. Mickey now holds numerous career Series records, including 18 home runs, 40 RBI and 42 runs scored. His lifetime homer total was 536. *Sweater, shirt insignia, socks, cap: navy blue.*

Roberto Clemente (1934–1972) was drafted by Pittsburgh from the Dodgers in 1954 and entered the Pirate outfield in 1955. He remained there for eighteen seasons. He batted over .300 thirteen times, with a high of .357 in 1967. He led the NL in batting four times, twice in hits. In 1966 he was named NL MVP. In the 1971 World Series, Clemente hit safely in every game for a batting average of .414. In 1972, his final season, hampered by injuries, he still managed to hit .312 and drive out his 3,000th hit. Tragedy struck shortly after the 1972 season: while he was flying on a mission of mercy to earthquake-torn Nicaragua, his plane crashed on takeoff and he was killed. *Shirt writing; cap letter; visor; sweater; second and fourth sock, top sleeve and top waist stripes: black. Helmet; collar; top sock, bottom sleeve and bottom waist (thin) stripes: golden yellow.*

Bob Gibson (born 1935) was a hard-throwing right-handed pitcher for the St. Louis Cardinals from 1959 through 1975. His finest year was 1968, at the height of the 1960s' pitching dominance, when he posted a 1.12 ERA along with 13 shutouts. Bob won 20 or better five times, with a high of 23 in 1970. He was a superb strikeout artist: he had nine years with more than 200 and a career total of 3,117. In the World Series' of 1964, 1967 and 1968, he set a record by winning 7 straight games. Overall, in Series play, he was 7-2, completed 8 of 9 starts and struck out 92 in 81 innings (compare with Whitey Ford's record of 94 accomplished in 146 innings for the Yanks). *Sweater; socks; cap; shirt bird, lettering and number: red. Bat design on shirt: yellow.*

Sandy Koufax (born 1935) was a left-handed pitcher for the Los Angeles Dodgers. In 1961 he won 18 and lost 13, leading the NL with 269 strikeouts. During the next five years, he won 111 and lost 34, a .766 winning percentage. His record in 1962-1966 was 14-7, 25-5, 19-5, 26-8 and 27-9. He won the Cy Young Award three times as the best pitcher in the majors. In 1965 he set an NL record with 382 strikeouts. His 11 shutouts in 1963 led the league and set the left-handed record. Arthritis forced him to retire after the 1966 season. Koufax averaged better than 1 strikeout per inning throughout his career. *Shirt, pants: gray. Socks, sweater, cap, shirt lettering and number: navy blue.*

Lou Brock (born 1939) was an outfielder for the Cubs and Cardinals from 1961 to 1979. In 1974, at age thirty-five, he broke Maury Wills's record for stolen bases in a season with 118. He led the NL in swipes for seven of the previous eight years, twice topping 70. During his career, he garnered a then all-time record high of 938 purloined sacks. He set another record by pilfering 50 or more bases for twelve straight years. Lou also holds the World Series record for the highest batting average for a player in 20 or more games (.391). *Shirt art, number and lettering; collar; sleeve stripes; twin leg stripes; sweater; five-sided sock sections; first thin sock stripes: red. Shirt, pants: light blue. Second thin sock stripes: blue.*

Pete Rose (born 1941) came to the big leagues with Cincinnati in 1963 as a second baseman and eventually played the other two bases *and* left and right field, playing brilliantly at each. He led NL outfielders in fielding three times. Rose hit .300 or better from 1965 to 1981 (except 1974), picking up three batting titles along the way (1968, 1969 and 1973). He set a major league record by collecting over 200 hits ten times. He led in hits seven times and in doubles five times. Pete tied the NL record consecutive-game hitting streak of 44, the first to approach DiMaggio's 56-game record. Rose is the all-time hit champion with 4,256 and is second in doubles. *Collar, sweater, socks, flash stripe on shoes, sleeve stripe, shirt writing, waist stripes, helmet: red. Shirt, pants: gray.*

Tom Seaver (born 1944) was a right-handed pitcher for the Mets, Reds, White Sox and Red Sox. He was considered an artist at pitching, with an excellent fastball. Tom joined the New York Mets in 1967 and won 16 in each of his first two seasons. In 1969 Tom and the Mets won the World Series. That year Tom had a 25-7 season with a 2.21 ERA. His major league records include: most seasons with 200 or more strikeouts (ten), most consecutive seasons with 200 or more strikeouts (nine) and most consecutive strikeouts in a game (10). He led the NL in ERA three times and strikeouts five times. He won the Cy Young Award for best NL pitcher in 1969, 1973 and 1975. *Socks; shirt writing; flash stripe on shoes; sweater; sleeve and waist stripes; cap: red.*

Rod Carew (born 1945) was put on second base by the Minnesota Twins in 1967. In 1969 he hit .332 and came back in 1970 to hit .366. From 1973 through 1980, his batting average read .350, .364, .359, .331, .388, .333, .318 and .331. He won batting titles in 1969, 1972-1975, 1977 and 1978. Rod led the league three times in hits, with a high of 239 in 1977, and twice in triples. He also stole more than 30 bases four times, including stealing home sixteen times in his career. Rod, who joined the California Angels as a free agent in 1979, closed out his career in 1985 with a lifetime batting average of .328. Elected to Hall of Fame in 1991. *Visor, sweater, top sleeve stripes, inner leg piping, outer leg piping (right stripe), leggings (center band), undershirt collar, shoulder art: navy blue. Shoes, helmet, shirt writing, bottom sleeve stripes, waist stripe, shirt collar, outer leg piping (left): red.*

Jim Palmer (born 1945) was a right-handed pitcher for the Baltimore Orioles from 1965 to 1984. He won 15 games in 1966 and capped the season with a 6-0 shutout of the Dodgers in the World Series. The next year he developed arm problems and spent the better part of 1967 and 1968 in the minor leagues. In 1969 Jim recovered and made a startling comeback with a 16-4 record, including a no-hitter. He went on to win 20 or more games eight times in his career. Palmer won the Cy Young Award for best AL pitcher in 1973, 1975 and 1976. *Shirt writing, piping, legging, collar, flash stripe on shoe, outer sleeve stripe, cap insignia: orange. Left panel of cap, sweater: black.*

Reggie Jackson (born 1946) began playing with the Athletics in 1967. In 1969 he made a career high of 47 homers, 118 RBI and a league-leading 123 runs. Starting in 1971 he and the As were in five consecutive AL playoffs. In 1975 he was tied for the AL home run title with 36. He signed with the Yankees as a free agent in 1976. In 1977 he set a World Series record with 5 homers in 6 games, the last 4 in succession. In 1978 he hit .462 in the AL playoffs. He signed with the Angels in 1982 and led the team in homers in 1984 and 1985. 1987 saw Reggie return to the Athletics for his last year in the majors. Reggie finished up with 563 home runs, now thirteenth on the all-time list. *Flash stripe on shoes: white. Helmet, leggings, shirt writing, sweater: navy blue.*

Mike Schmidt (born 1949) was a third baseman for Philadelphia from 1972 to 1989. Between 1974 and 1986, Schmidt led the NL in home runs a record-breaking eight times, peaking in 1980 with 48. In nine seasons, he drove in over 100 runs, leading the NL four times (with a high of 121 in 1980). Mike also excelled in the 1980 World Series with 2 homers, 7 RBI and a .381 batting average, winning the World Series MVP award. The powerhouse behind a decade-long Phillies resurgence, Schmidt was named NL MVP in 1980, 1981 and 1986. *Three stripes on each shoe: white. Helmet; shoes; belt; leggings; side bar on leg, shirt and sleeve; sweater; shirt writing; pinstripes (trace over): red.*